Learn to Move!

# I ICE-SKATE!

By Bray Jacobson

Gareth Stevens
PUBLISHING

**Please visit our website, www.garethstevens.com. For a free color catalog of all our high-quality books, call toll free 1-800-542-2595 or fax 1-877-542-2596.**

**Library of Congress Cataloging-in-Publication Data**
Names: Jacobson, Bray, author.
Title: I ice-skate! / Bray Jacobson.
Other titles: I ice skate!
Description: Buffalo, New York : Gareth Stevens Publishing, [2025] | Series: Learn to move! | Includes index.
Identifiers: LCCN 2023045840 | ISBN 9781482466041 (library binding) | ISBN 9781482466034 (paperback) | ISBN 9781482466058 (ebook)
Subjects: LCSH: Skating–Juvenile literature. | Winter sports–Juvenile literature.
Classification: LCC GV849 .J334 2025 | DDC 796.91–dc23/eng/20231023
LC record available at https://lccn.loc.gov/2023045840

First Edition

Published in 2025 by
**Gareth Stevens Publishing**
2544 Clinton Street
Buffalo, NY 14224



Editor: Kristen Nelson
Designer: Leslie Taylor

Photo credits: Cover Maria Moroz/Shutterstock.com; p. 5 Nigmatulina Aleksandra/Shutterstock.com; pp. 7, 24 (ice rink & mittens) FatCamera/iStockphoto.com; p. 9, 24 (ice skates) Evgeny Bakharev/Shutterstock.com; pp. 11 Joy Brown/Shutterstock.com; p. 13 SeventyFour/iStockphoto.com; p. 15 ArtMarie/iStockphoto.com; p. 17 AleksandarNakic/iStockphoto.com; p. 19 BlueOrange Studio/Shutterstock.com; p. 21 kali9/iStockphoto.com; p. 23 fotosparrow/Shutterstock.com.



Printed in the United States of America

CPSIA compliance information: Batch #CS25GS: For further information contact Gareth Stevens, New York, New York at 1-800-542-2595.

# Contents

It is time for my
ice-skating lesson!

It is cold at the ice rink.
I wear a coat.
I wear mittens.

I put on my ice skates.
They are white.
I tie them tight.

I see my friend Jorge.
He wears hockey skates.
They are black.

Miss Tanya teaches the class.
We warm up.
We stretch.

Miss Tanya teaches us how to fall!
Frank tries first.

The ice is slippery.
It is hard to get back up!

Next we learn to glide.
Kara can do it!
She glides on one foot.

We play tag on the ice!
Luke is fast.
He tags Jenna!

I watch the older skaters.
I cannot wait
to skate more!

# Words to Know

ice rink

ice skates

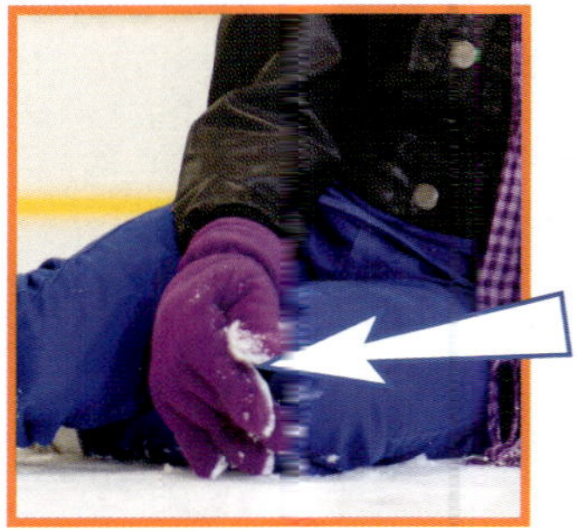

mittens

# Index